AVIATION PC

CU00758434

BRI`..._..
AIRFIELD BUILDINGS
VOLUME 2
THE EXPANSION &
INTER-WAR PERIODS

Graham Buchan Innes

Midland Publishing

Dedicated to Sgt David Noble (1365070)
Wireless Operator/Air Gunner, 38 Sqn RAF,
shot down, missing, presumed killed,
Middle East, 26th October 1942.

© 2000 Graham Buchan Innes
ISBN 1 85780 101 6

Published by Midland Publishing
24 The Hollow, Earl Shilton
Leicester, LE9 7NA, England
Tel: 01455 847 815   Fax: 01455 841 805
E-mail: midlandbooks@compuserve.com

Midland Publishing is an imprint of
Ian Allan Publishing Ltd

Worldwide distribution (except North America):
Midland Counties Publications
Unit 3, Maizefield, Hinckley Fields
Hinckley, Leics., LE10 1YF, Great Britain
Tel: 01455 233 747   Fax: 01455 233 737
E-mail: midlandbooks@compuserve.com

North American trade distribution:
Specialty Press Publishers & Wholesalers Inc.
11605 Kost Dam Road, North Branch, MN 55056
Tel: 651 583 3239   Fax: 651 583 2023
Toll free telephone: 800 895 4585

Design concept and layout
© 2000 Midland Publishing

Printed in England by
Ian Allan Printing Ltd
Riverdene Business Park, Molesey Road,
Hersham, Surrey, KT12 4RG

CONTENTS

Title page illustration

Officers' Mess – 3935/35 – RAF Manby
One of the larger types of Officers' Mess of the
period, it had three levels with two large wings.
It is thought that the drawing number covers
the wings also, whereas with some of the
smaller Messes the wings were added with
their own drawing numbers. The Mess at
Shawbury, in my earlier volume, whilst looking
virtually the same, is now thought to be a
3653/36. The 3935 was designed for 107
married Officers and 84 singles.

PREFACE

Since my first volume 'British Airfield Buildings of the Second World War' was published, much more interest seems to have been generated. During research for my first book, my travels took me across the country visiting dozens of temporary airfields with a few of the permanent stations included for comparison.

This second book is primarily focused on the Expansion Period, from 1935 to 1939, when the majority of the buildings were permanent. However other inter-war buildings are also included. Some stations, such as armament and observer training schools, for example RAF Jurby, were started during the Expansion Period but had 90% temporary buildings. A handful of First World War and post First World War buildings are also included, as well as some wartime temporary designs for comparison. It is important to remind readers that the early airfields and Expansion Period airfields had most of their buildings grouped together, including the Living, Technical and Domestic sites. Only during the Second World War, generally speaking, did the Air Ministry adopt a policy of dispersal.

The majority of the buildings In this volume were of a standard type design and although they are pictured at a certain location, they will of course be extant at many other locations across the country. It is interesting to note that the Royal Air Force had many stations overseas, even before the outbreak of the Second World War and at many of these stations, standard designs were also utilised, albeit some with modifications. Countries where buildings may still be extant include Egypt, Palestine, Kenya, Aden, Sudan, Malta, Gibraltar, Malaya and Iraq.

During the inter-war period, the possibility of the invasion of Britain was not properly considered and therefore Battle HQs and pillboxes did not appear in any significant number until 1941. Defensive positions too, did not appear in abundance until well into the war. A more comprehensive coverage of these, along with Naval buildings is in my earlier volume.

Officers' Mess – 3935/35 – RAF Manby
This grand Neo-Georgian entrance was typical of the Expansion Period Officers' Mess. Manby is a very good example of an Expansion Period airfield, unlike most of the other disused airfields in 'Nissen County'.

Expansion Period

The Expansion Period started in earnest in 1935 after the Air Ministry Works Directorate had been established earlier in the 1930s. The threat of Hitler alone had persuaded the Air Ministry into this great expansion.

Stations like Biggin Hill and Duxford had already been upgraded in the 1920s and '30s, but this new period was to build many new stations as well as upgrade many existing First World War stations. The Nazi threat had become very great and the need for more new and updated airfields was greater than ever.

Some airfields had been upgraded to Expansion Period standard by the start or just after the start of the war, but others, particularly airfields which had been started from scratch, were not completed until later in the war; examples of this were Middle Wallop and High Ercall. Examples of the first Expansion Period upgrades were to be found at Upper Heyford, Odiham, Harwell, Cranwell and Leuchars, whilst examples of new Expansion Period stations could be found at Finningley, Dishforth, Upwood and Hullavington. Many Aircraft Storage Units and Maintenance Units were also established on these permanent stations. Along with the Expansion Period came many hundreds of standard building designs to be used across the country. These standard designs were often 'flat roofed' as well as traditionally tiled.

Early expansion control towers were the 'Fort' types, their design numbers being 1959/34 and the concrete version, the 207/36. These 'Fort' type control towers or watch offices were the most common of the earlier standard designs and examples can still be seen at numerous airfields including Catterick and Cosford. Other Towers from the Expansion Period included the 'Villa' 5845/39 and the 'Chief Flying Instructors Block' 5740/36. Hangarage was also to be very much more standardised, although there had been earlier standard type hangars such as the General Service Shed of 1916 and the 'A' type hangar from the 1920s.

The 'C' hangars were probably the most numerous type of all the Expansion Period aircraft sheds. The early 'C' hangars had extensive brickwork, particularly at the ends. The 'C' hangars could be 'hipped' with sloping sides to the transversed roof, or 'gabled', with flat gable ends, the latter being fairly rare. Later this design was replaced by the less labour intensive and cheaper to build Austerity C hangar, which was basically the same shape but did not have the mass of brickwork at the ends. The even simpler 'C1' had asbestos sheet cladding replacing much of the side brickwork. A common design number for the early 'C' hangar was 2029/34, although there were many updated and different sized versions all with their own drawing numbers. One of the good things about these standard hangar designs was that they could be built in various sizes, each having as many aircraft bays as was dictated by the Air Ministry.

At Catterick, examples of small and large 'C' hangars can still be seen side by side. Other common designs included the 'D' hangar, 2312-3/36, the 'L' shed, 10755/39 both favourites of Storage and Maintenance Units. The 'F' shed, 7904/36, and the 'J' hangar, 5836/39, were other designs that could be found across the country. Transportable hangars such as the 'Bellman' were actually designed between the wars and these too were used to complement the permanent hangars. During the war years the transportable hangar really came in to its own with its ease of erection and low cost and as a result, many new transportable hangar designs appeared. Included in these were the 'T1' hangar, 7541/41, the 'T2', 3653/42 and the 'Robins' hangar, 2204/41.

The standardisation of many other buildings was now commonplace, Heating Stations, Water Towers, Photographic Blocks and Messes to name but a few. The famous 'Neo-Georgian' style Officers' Mess is probably the most remembered of the standard designs, although many were modified or had extra storeys. From 1937 many standard designs would include protection from penetration and explosive effect. These buildings were often referred to as 'Protected'. This protection normally meant the incorporation of reinforced concrete, and this, along with a shortage of materials led to a plethora of flat-roofed buildings. Towards the end of the Expansion Period and after the outbreak of war the Air Ministry adopted a policy of dispersal. Having nearly every building grouped together, as was the case at the Expansion airfields, provided too easy a target for the enemy. Nearly all the new temporary stations would have to be built with their various sites dispersed, sometimes across miles and miles.

In a few cases where airfields of the Expansion Period were to be used for Auxiliary or Volunteer Reserve duties, these airfields would have been generally of a temporary nature. Examples of this can be found at Dyce and Jurby. Compare in the book, the difference between the temporary buildings at Jurby with the other Expansion Period buildings.

Book Format

Although strictly speaking, the inter-war and Expansion Period airfields did not have their various sites dispersed, buildings of a similar purpose were generally grouped together within the one big site. For this reason I have continued to use the format of the first book 'British Airfield Buildings of the Second World War'. The buildings are grouped into three sections, roughly in the areas where you would expect to find them. Of course in some cases buildings could be found at various locations, such as latrines. Geographical unsuitability also meant some buildings being 'out of position'. Included again, where known, is the design number and year, for instance 1959/34, where 1959 is the Air Ministry design drawing number and the year is 1934.

A brief description of the building's use is included where required and any known modifications are also pointed out. The use of many of these buildings has already been covered in the earlier book, so any information not in this volume will probably be found there.

The subject of airfield buildings is so large that coverage of every pattern could not be achieved, but every attempt has been made to include the most popular designs.

Photographs

All photographs are by the author, with the exception of the following:
Bob Woolnough (Leuchars Tower) page 7; David E Thompson, (Watton and Waterbeach towers) pages 8 and 11.

Acknowledgements

Station Commander, RAF Waddington; Station Commander, RAF Shawbury; Station Commander, RAF Sealand; Squadron Leader A Clark, RAF Newton; HQ Logistic Command, RAF Brampton; The Staff of RAF Scampton; The Staff of RAF Upwood (now closed); The Defence Land Agency; 1st Battalion, 22nd Cheshire Regiment, Oakington; 21st Signal Regiment, Air Support, Azimghur Barracks, Colerne; 1st Battalion, Royal Regiment of Wales, Clive Barracks, Ternhill; 3rd Regiment, Royal Horse Artillery, Allenbrooke Barracks, Topcliffe; The School of Defence Transport, Normandy Barracks, Leconfield; The Staff of the RAF Museum Archive, Hendon; Lucas Ltd, Fradley Distribution Centre, Lichfield; Rolls-Royce, Hucknall; Bastion Security, Swinderby; The Ulster Aviation Society, Langford Lodge; Aeroplane Collection, Hooton Park (now closed); Dave Smith; Paul Francis; Graham Crisp

Select Bibliography

British Airfield Buildings of the Second World War; Innes, Midland Publishing.
Britain's Military Airfields, 1939-1945, Smith, PSL.
Control Towers, Francis, Airfield Research Publishing.
British Military Airfield Architecture, Francis, PSL.
Action Stations, volumes 1 to 10, various authors, PSL.
20th Century Defences in Britain, Handbook of the 'Defence of Britain' project, (Council for British Archaeology)
The Royal Air Force Builds for War, The Stationery Office.
Airfield Review, Magazine of the Airfield Research Group.

For readers who wish to learn more about airfields and airfield buildings, then the *Airfield Research Group* is well recommended, publishing an excellent quarterly magazine, full of news and articles.
Details from: Raymond Towler, 33a Earl Street Thetford, Norfolk, IP24 2AB.
Telephone: 01842 765 399. E-mail: R.T.@btinternet.com

Amendments and updates for Volume 1

page 12 top: Temporary brick construction.
page 14 top: Brick version is numbered 5845/39.
page 18 top: RSJ, *Rolled* Steel Joints.
page 19 bottom: Now demolished.
page 21 top: Drawing number 232/14.
page 27 top and bottom: Both are *'Main'* Hangars.
page 34 top and bottom: Both are *'Robins'* Hangars.
page 43 bottom: Drawing 12411/41.
page 59 bottom: Drawing 2048-9/34.
page 62 top: Drawing 1739/41.
page 76 bottom: The function of this building is now uncertain.
page 112 top and bottom: Now demolished.
page 113 bottom: Drawing number should read 2948/34.
page 115 bottom: Now demolished.
page 119 bottom: This SSQ annex is actually the Decontamination Centre.

Part 1

Airfield Site Buildings

Watch Office with Meteorological Section – 2328/39 – RAF Leuchars
Note the rendered brickwork and the added 'Portacabin' to the roof.

the first floor control room. This design was the first real attempt to standardise Expansion Period Watch Offices. In a few cases the first floor observation tower was removed and a whole new control room with balcony was added across the full width of the building. The drawing number for this was 4698/43 and examples were at Leconfield, Scampton and Harwell.

An example of the 'Fort' tower at Cosford is still used for Air Traffic Control.

'Fort' Watch Office – 1959/34 – RAF Bicester
The most common of the inter-war period Control Towers/Watch Offices, the 'Fort' had two design types. The 1959/34 was built of brick; the concrete version was the 207/36. 'Fort' Watch Offices could be found at about 40 stations, including Honington, Finningley, Cottesmore, Catterick, Mildenhall, Waddington and Bircham Newton. On the ground floor were toilets, rest room and watch office. A spiral staircase led to

If you have a specific interest in Air Traffic Control and control towers, then the book *Control Towers* by Paul Francis is a must.

Fort Watch Office – 207/36 – RAF Watton
Rear, side view of this, the concrete version.

Watch Office – 207/36 with 4698/43 conversion – RAF West Raynham

Watch Office – 207/36, 4698/43 – RAF Hemswell
This tower has also had the 4698/43 conversion, which was basically the removal of the central tower and the addition of a new control room. (centre left in picture). This tower has also had a later extension to the right side.

Watch Office – 207/36, 4698/43, 5871c/55 – RAF Leconfield
This is a good example of 'Tower Evolution', showing the 207/36 bottom left, the 4698/43 modification centre left and post-war extensions to the right, with a 5871c/55 added to the top.

Watch Office with Meteorological Section 'Villa' – 5845/39 – RAF Swinderby
This, along with the concrete version (2328/39), is what was probably the second most common tower designed during the Expansion Period, with around thirty being built. Stations to have these towers included Swanton Morley, Colerne, Abingdon, Oakington and Middleton St George. The first floor frontage windows have been reduced in size and a small porch added to the ground floor.

Watch Office with Meteorological Section – 5845/39 – RAF Waterbeach
The first floor frontage windows have been modernised on this one.

Watch Office with Met Section 'Villa' – 2328/39 – RAF Topcliffe
The Visual Control room on this one has been added later, along with the
added modification to the right on the ground floor. The 2328 was a concrete
copy of the brick built 5845/39. On the ground floor would have been the Met
Office, Watch Office and toilets, whilst on the first floor was the Control room
and Signals office. The internal layout was almost identical to the wartime
design 518/40; indeed a distinguishing feature of both is the protruding stairwell
to the rear. The Villa had rounded corners to the frontage. Other examples were
at Leuchars, Leeming, Linton-on-Ouse, Lindholme and Waddington.

Watch Office with Met Section – 5845/39, 5871c/55 – RAF Oakington
This standard Villa has had a new Visual Control Room added 5871c/55. Other
types of watch office would also have this later addition, including the 343/43
at Watton, the 343/43 at Kinloss and the 518/40 at Pershore.

Watch Office for SLG – SLG – Wath Head
This Ministry of Aircraft Production rudimentary type watch office had two
rectangular sections connected by a narrower corridor section. Other
examples could be found at Ollerton and Bodorgan.

Chief Flying Instructors Block – 5740/36 – RAF Shawbury
This substantial Watch Office/Control Tower was present at only a handful
of other stations, namely South Cerney, Ternhill, Hullavington and Little
Rissington. It resembles an oversized 'Fort' tower, with an extra storey. The
Chief Flying Instructors at Shawbury were still using this building in 1996. The
station is now the home of a helicopter pilot training school.

Chief Flying Instructors Block – 5740/36 – RAF Ternhill
In this rear view one can see how the original observation post on the second
floor has been removed to make way for a new VCR. This tower is often referred
to as the FTS tower, because it was found only at Flying Training Schools.

Fighter Satellite Watch Office – 3156/41, 1536/42 – RAF Ludham
This rudimentary watch office has been upgraded to include a switch room, 1536/42, the small extension to the left. The basic 3156/41 was an updated version of the 17658/40, looking identical externally. The 3156 could be found at numerous locations including Fordoun, Great Orton and Lulsgate, whilst the 17658 could be found at Stapleford Tawney, North Weald and Fowlmere.

Night Fighter Watch Office – FCW4514 (12096/41) – RAF Charmy Down
Looking rather similar to the 12779/41, the window sizes varied from station to station, as is the case with other tower designs. A feature of this type was concrete beams above the windows spanning the entire building width. Other stations to have this tower were Kingscliffe, Darley Moor, Melbourne, and Hibaldstow. None of the other towers in this group appear to have the brick erection on top of the roof.

Watch Office and Squadron Office – DX698/? – RAF Duxford
This early watch office was basic hutting with a few extra windows. This
example was fairly representative of first World War Watch Offices and it is
believed that this one dates from 1917. This example was replaced during the
war by a 12779/41, which is still used today. Another First World War type was
the 'Control Tops', which would have been positioned at the top, or to the side
of one of the brick gantries on 'General Service Sheds'

Watch Office – RAF Langford Lodge
This unusual tower is believed to be one of the first in the UK to have angled
windows to cut down on reflections. The exact drawing number is not known,
but the design may have been for the Ministry of Aircraft Production or indeed
American. The Ulster Aviation Society are presently trying to refurbish this
building to its original condition.

Watch Office – 756/36 – RAF Manby
This inter-war Watch Office would appear to be a 'one-off'. It was replaced in
the 1950s with an up-to-date tower, the 2548/55. Note the 'C' hangar in the
background.

Civil Tower – Barton/Manchester
Although much larger, this civil tower from the inter-war period (circa 1934),
can be compared with the RAF 'Fort' of similar vintage. Barton airfield was
actually used to train RAF volunteer reserves and for a short period was
therefore an RAF station in its own right.

'C' Hangar (Hipped) – 4292/35 – RAF Manby
Here we have one of the five 'C' hangars at Manby, all having different drawing numbers. These different design numbers normally refer either to the amount of aircraft bays, (hangar size), or to the side office, workshop accommodation. Note, the windows at the top of the sliding doors have been painted over. From 1936, most were built of reinforced concrete.

'C' Hangar (Hipped) – 2029/34 – RAF Silloth

'C' Hangar (Gabled) – RAF Aldergrove
The difference in the 'Gabled' version can be clearly seen, with the flat gable ends to the transversed roof. Sealand also has extant examples which are numbered 2134/24 on the site plan.

Aircraft Repair Shed 'C' Hangar (Hipped) – RAF Shawbury
The 'C' hangar pictured here is one of the smaller 'C' types and is more slender than the normal 'C'. It was used for aircraft repair as opposed to just storage. The workshops and test bays to the side were peculiar to the Aircraft Repair Shed and are clearly seen in this shot. Note, only four sliding doors across the frontage as opposed to six on the normal 'C' hangars and they can still be seen at Catterick, Wittering, Little Rissington and Manby.

'C' Hangar (Protected) – RAF Ternhill
Compare this protected 'C' hangar with the earlier Hipped 'C' hangar in the background. The extensive brickwork at the ends has been dispensed with. The large side windows on these large hangars served to disperse the blast if an incendiary should come through the roof and thus limit damage to the hangar and its contents. Many fine specimens can still be found across the country. These hangars were often referred to as 'C1' or Type C Protected. AMWD numbers include 8180/38 and 5533/39.

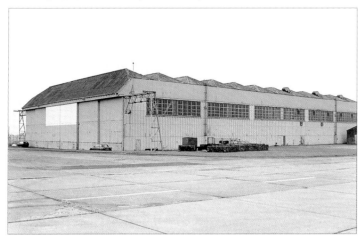

'C' Hangar (Unprotected) – RAF Aldergrove
Compare this later 'C' hangar to the 'C' protected above. Much of the brickwork and concrete has been replaced by asbestos sheets, saving on manpower and raw materials.

General Service Shed (circa 1916) – RAF Tadcaster
This First World War shed was very common in its day and many stations were still using them well after the Second World War. The RAF pulled out of RAF Tadcaster/RFC Bramham Moor after the First World War, but this example was still extant in 1997, being used by an agricultural college as a grain and equipment store. Among the many other stations to have these were Yatesbury, Beverley and Montrose. Many General Service sheds built after 1917 incorporated the 'Belfast Truss' in their construction. These hangars employed wooden side braces, seen clearly here.

Coupled General Service Sheds – 332/17 (377/17) – RAF Hooton Park
The 332/17 was a far more substantial design, incorporating a lot of brickwork. The truss braces are also of brick. The examples at Hooton Park are shown on the site plan as 377/17. They are however believed to be 332/17 but with slightly differing brickwork. Numerous can still be seen including Duxford, Bracebridge Heath, Leuchars and Sealand.

'F' Shed – RAF Aldergrove
This side-opening hangar has recently been reclad and is unusual as it has extensive brickwork to the ends; the 'F' normally had steel cladding all the way round. The 'F' shed can be traced back to the First World War, but drawing numbers for this era are unconfirmed. Some were later re-erected as the 7904/36. Others could be found at Pembrey, Stormy Down, Evanton and Jurby.

Equipment Depot Stores – RAF Langford Lodge
At Langford this building was used as the Main Machine Shop and is based on the 'Equipment Depot Stores'. Ten similar buildings were also at Burtonwood Repair Depot (BRD). They formed two parallel lines, two sets of four coupled together, with two singles at one end. These buildings were used for aircraft assembly, modification, overhaul and general storage. The manufacture of propellers, canopies, and many other factory processes would take place. The Ulster Aviation Society house their aircraft collection in the one pictured above.

'A' Hangar – 19a/24 – RAF Silloth
The 'A' was the standard permanent hangar of the 1920s and '30s and was very similar to the 'C' gabled, but without the extensive brickwork. The 'A' can still be seen at numerous sites including Netheravon and North Weald. It is thought that the general pattern for the 'A' was 19/24 but it is annotated on various site plans with differing numbers, as it could be built to various lengths.

'A' Hangar – RAF Catfoss
This side shot shows the transversed and gabled roof layout and the distinctive access gantry along the side.

'J' Hangar – 5836/39 – RAF Holme-upon-Spalding Moor
Recognisable by its curved steel roof and sloping steel roof braces, the 'K' Hangar 3084/39 looks externally to be identical but the 'J' was set up internally for operational use. A site plan is required to distinguish the two apart. Specimens are still extant at Goxhill, Edzell and Burtonwood. The building in the foreground in this shot is unidentified.

'K' Hangar – 3084/39 – RAF Lichfield
The 'K' seemed to be more a favourite with Maintenance Units and Aircraft Servicing Units.

Bellman Hangars – 8349/37 – RAF Baginton
This was the standard transportable shed of the era and with 400 erected many can still be seen across the country.

Bellman Hangars – 8349/37 – RAF Hucknall (Rolls-Royce)
Seen here are two different sizes side by side. The one on the left has only two thirds the clear door height of the one on the right.

'J' Hangar – 5836/39 – RAF Colerne
This example shows clearly a later modification above the doors to accommodate aircraft with larger tails. This type of modification can also be seen at Middleton St George and Kinloss. The 'Gaydon' hangar from the 1950s had this type of entrance as standard. See below.

'Gaydon' Hangar – RAF Coningsby
The 'Gaydon' hangar was a 1950s design, probably based on the earlier 'J' and 'K' hangars, although it was much larger. The 'Gaydon' takes its name from RAF Gaydon which supplemented the hangars it already had with the 'Gaydon' type which could accommodate aircraft of the V-Force. Compare it with the standard 'J' seen to its left. This type of hangar can also be seen at RAF Valley.

Super Robins Hangar Type 'A' – 2243/41 – RAF Lossiemouth
This small hangar of the war years was very common. Not only was it found on airfield sites but on many dispersed sites at MUs and ASUs. Stations with extant examples include Penkridge and Shawbury.

'L' Shed – RAF Burtonwood
This hangar, like the 'D' hangar, was to be found mainly at Storage and Maintenance units. Looking indeed like an enlarged and elongated Blister hangar, it was sometimes covered in grass. The 'L' shed was of concrete construction and had various design numbers, including 5163/39 and 10755/39. There was also a version which incorporated steel reinforcement and this was known as the 'E' shed 7305/37, which can be seen on page 26. Both the 'L' and the 'E' were upgraded versions of the earlier and less popular 'Lamella' 6953/36. Less than 30 'Lamellas' were built, compared with over 100 'L's and nearly 50 'E's.

'E' Shed – 7305/37 – RAF Hullavington
Compare the doors and extended concrete door gantries, which the 'L' did not have. The entrance at the other end is much smaller with only two doors and no extended gantries. Amongst the airfields to still have them is Aston Down.

'D' Hangar – 2312-3/36 – RAF Cosford
This MU and ASU hangar is now part of the museum at Cosford and still boasts a fine collection of 1930s and '40s aircraft, Note the unusual concrete gantries. The examples at St Athan and Brize Norton are still being used more or less for their original purpose.

'D' Hangar – 2312-3/36 – RAF Silloth

Like many 'L' sheds, the 'D' hangar would often have specialist annexes attached or nearby, that were associated with the erection, maintenance and reprocessing of aircraft.

Hangar Dimensions

Below is a list of common hangar sizes based on the standard designs. Sizes of the larger hangars vary according to the amount of aircraft bays. The most common in each case has been included. Dimensions are in feet (width x length x overall height), rounded to the nearest foot. The widths of the larger hangars, do not include side annexes, which were 17 feet wide for the 'C' hangar and 23 feet wide for the 'J' and 'K' hangars.

Permanent Hangars	Drawing no.	Dimensions	Notes
'C'	2029/34	150 x 300 x 52	12 x 25 Bays
'A'	19a/24	120 x 250 x 43	
'D'	2312/36	150 x 300 x 52	concrete gantries
'J'/'K'	5836/39, 3084/39	151 x 300 x 49	curved steel roof
'L'/'E'	10755/39, 7305/37	160 x 300 x 36	blister shaped

Temporary and Transportable Hangars			
'T1'	7541/41	97 x 175 x 37	shallow gable end
'T2'	8254/40	121 x 240 x 39	shallow gable end
'Bellman'	8349/37	95 x 175 x 34	shallow gable end
'B1'	11776/41	120 x 227 x 35	high gable end
'Callender Hamilton'	17346/40	100 x 185 x 35	
'Robins type B'	2204/41	44 x 62 x 24	sloping sides
'Super Robins type A'	2243/41	60 x 72 x 28	sloping sides
'Teeside S1'	12819/40	60 x 50 x 26	shallow gable end
'Miskin Blister (Over)'	12512/41	65 x 45 x 20	
'Dorman Long Blister'	4630/42	90 x 45 x 20	

Machine Gun Post – Type 25 – RAF West Raynham
This small machine gun post is believed to be a Type 25. The only other known 'round' MG Posts were the 'Pickett-Hamilton' Fort and the prefabricated concrete 'Norcon'.

Machine Gun Post – Type 22 – RAF Oakington
This small MG Post was less than half the size of the type 27, which was also hexagonal. Both types were common at Expansion Period airfields.

4 Bay Petrol Tanker Shed – 4157/35 – RAF Upwood
The concrete 4157/35 came in various sizes and along with the brick version below, was the standard inter-war tender shed.

6 Bay Petrol Tanker Shed – 2773/34 – RAF Duxford
Like the above, this 6 bay version could be found all over the country at Expansion airfields. Also seen to the right of the picture is the side rear of the 4982/38 Stop Butts. The support buttresses can be clearly seen.

Night Flying Equipment Store – RAF Topcliffe
Night flying equipment such as gooseneck flares and their trolley etc. would be stored here. The Night flying Shed nearly always enjoyed a good position next to the Tower. In this picture, you can see the strange roof design technique used In many Expansion buildings.

Night Flying Equipment Store – 3235/39 – RAF Colerne
Brick version of the above.

Night Flying Equipment Store – 12411/41 – RAF Elvington
This was the most common of the wartime NFE stores; gooseneck flares,
Glim lamps and Illuminated Landing Tee would all be stored here. This is one
of a handful of preserved buildings at the excellent Yorkshire Air Museum at
Elvington.

Operational wall art – RAF Elvington
Seen on the back wall inside the NFE store at Elvington is this detailed airfield
plan. The runways and dispersals are all numbered. The plan would have been
used as an *aide-mémoire* by airmen before setting of to lay the goosenecks etc.

Fire Tender Shed – RAF Topcliffe
Looking very much like the 2773/34 Petrol Tender Shed and the NFE store, its position and size should give it away. It should be near the tower and normally have no more than two bays. The NFE store normally had three bays. The tanker sheds were usually nearer the Technical site. The right hand door on this example has been bricked up.

Meteorological Office and Briefing Office – 1943/36 – RAF Manby
The Met Office would normally have been in the Tower, but Manby, being an extremely busy flying station, needed a larger than normal example.

Pyrotechnic Store (Ready Use)
4264/35 – RAF Upwood
Pyrotechnics is basically a posh name for flares etc. The Pyro store was to be found at all stations. They all looked basically the same, but there were many different drawing numbers, the 4264/35 being fairly popular.

Pyrotechnic Store (Ready Use)
3800/38 – RAF Jurby
Compare this one with the one above. Extra safety-locking bars are a feature on this example.

Magazine/Pyrotechnic Store – 2801/37 – RAF West Raynham
This design was typical of buildings used for the storage of explosive materials. An internal brick storeroom would be surrounded by reinforced concrete and earth banked up against the concrete walls. This afforded the best protection from a blast.

Magazine – 4279/37 – RAF Manby

Fusing Point (Ultra-Heavy) – 7900/42 – RAF West Raynham
This semi-sunken Nissen fusing point was fairly standard on bomb dumps during the war. They were often added to existing bomb dumps as war operations became more extensive.

Incendiary and Pyrotechnics Store – 1003/37 – RAF West Raynham
These bomb stores came in varying sizes but by far the most popular was the three bay like this one.

Incendiary Bomb and Pyrotechnics Store – 18185/40 – RAF Tatenhill
This three bay store from 1940 can be compared with the preceding
Expansion example. Strangely, It incorporates nearly all brickwork as opposed
to the cheaper and more readily available concrete.

Aircraft Test Butt – 4019/37 – RAF Jurby
Aircraft would test their cannon by firing into the recess, which would have a
sloping bank of sand. The wartime equivalent was very similar, having all the
same features.

Aircraft Test Butt – 4982/38 – RAF Duxford

Shooting Butts/Rifle Range – RAF Duxford
All rifle ranges or shooting butts are basically the same, the main features being a large back wall with a traversed bank of sand to slow down and stop the shells safely. Targets would be placed in or immediately in front of the sand. At the other end was a hutment from which to fire. These common constructions are still used today.

Rifle Range/Test Butt – 3958/37 – RAF Upwood
This was the concrete version of the standard Butts and could be found across the country. It is almost identical to the wartime designs.

Part 2

Technical and Instructional Site Buildings

Armoury – 7616/37 – RAF Scampton
Standard concrete armoury.

Parachute Store – 1971/34 – RAF Manby
The parachutes would be checked and packed in this small purpose-built
building, the small dormer affording more light and space for the pulleys, used
to hang the parachutes for inspection and repair, in the roof space. This type
was one of the most popular of the Expansion Period designs along with those
that follow.

Parachute Store – 1971/34 – RAF Waddington
An example of this type of building at Shawbury was still being used for the
preparation of parachutes in 1996.

Parachute Store – 175/36 – RAF Newton
This concrete store was present at many of the later Expansion airfields, these stations relying more heavily on pre-cast concrete structures. Compare it to the 1971/34. It has only three large windows to the side and has a flat roof extension where the dormer would be. This example has a modification to the rear, not seen in this shot.

Parachute Store – RAF Colerne
This is a brick version of the above. This one has been rendered and has a 'Seco' extension to the rear. The site plan shows it to be a 6351/37, but is unconfirmed.

Parachute Store – 1550/36 – RAF Jurby
This was a temporary Air Ministry Timber Hutting store. However, the similarity between It and other parachute stores can easily be seen.

Parachute Store – 1550/36 (R) and W1139/41 (L) – RAF Jurby
As Jurby got busier during the war, the old wooden store was supplemented with another store which was a hybrid of temporary brick and Nissen hutting. Like most other temporary brick buildings, this one has been rendered.

Dinghy Shed/Store – 4303/43 – RAF West Raynham
The dinghy shed never really appeared until well into the war, although dinghies had been packed, checked and stored in other multi-purpose buildings previously.

Rest Room and Battery Charging Room – 4082/36 – RAF Duxford
This is a rather strange combination.

Main Stores – 2057/34 – RAF Waddington
This building cannot be mistaken for any other with its raised fabric store in the centre. This, one of the most popular store designs, was to be found at many locations including Little Rissington. This example has been greatly modified, the centre door being reduced and new extensions added to either side.

Main Stores – 7064/37 – RAF Swinderby
Other numbers for this standard style include 4287/35 and 2056/34.

Main Stores (L) – 840/30, Workshops (R) – 814/30 – RAF Hendon

Main Stores – 808/27 – RAF Hucknall

Main Stores (circa 1925) – RAF Bicester
Bicester actually had its own railway spur which led right here to the main stores.

Workshops, Parachute Store, Oil and Dope Store – 286/17 – RAF Duxford
During the First World War the parachute store was housed in this multi-purpose building. The importance and necessity of the parachute would soon make it worthy of its own specialised store.

Lubricants and Inflammables Store – RAF Swinderby
This building can be recognised by its small raised windows with louvres
above. The doors are of protective steel.

Lubricants and Inflammables Store – 1967/34 – RAF Ternhill
This type of 'L & I' store could be found at many Expansion Period airfields, the
example at Manby having an extra window to the side.

Lubricants and Inflammables Store – 3800/38 – RAF Jurby
This temporary wooden version did not afford a lot of protection for its
contents. Seen on the right hand side of the building is a long bench. Probably
not the safest of places to sit down for a smoke!

Lubricants Store – 329/26 – RAF Bicester

Fuel Store – 191-3/28 – RAF Bicester

Fuel Store – RAF Waddington
A standard design, but with unusual buttressing added to the walls. Standard
designs of fuel store did not normally have this. (eg 4166/35 at West Raynham)

Station Workshops – 6957/37 – RAF Colerne
This common building was originally designed to house an engine repair shop to the left and an airframe repair shop to the right. In the centre would be a welding shop, machine shop and a blacksmiths. As a general purpose building, the specific use of this design was often changed to suite a particular station's needs. One of its more common uses was as a Mechanical Transport servicing building. Both main doors have been bricked up on this example. Another design which was virtually the same was the 2048/34, one of which could be seen at the former RAF station at Harwell.

Workshops and Ground Servicing – 4923/35 – RAF Topcliffe
Basically this was a concrete version of the above. A lack of raw materials including bricks meant that many standard designs would have to be built of concrete. This shot shows the left hand side of the workshops and the concrete sections are clearly visible.

Workshops – 288/17 – RAF Duxford

Workshops – 1788/25 – RAF Bicester

Engine Test House (3 Bay) – 702/26 – RAF Bicester
This building was also to be found at many of the earlier stations. Indeed a two bay version may still be seen at Hendon.

Aero Engine Test Bay – 8800/38 – RAF Shawbury
Bircham Newton also had one of these buildings although it had the side workshops to the right. It is unclear why, but this example at Shawbury has a huge blast protection wall behind it.

Gunnery Workshops (L) and Respirator Workshops (R) – 293/17
RAF Duxford

Latrines and Ablutions – 534/17 – RAF Duxford

Technical Latrines – RAF Bicester
This 'little room' was to be found at all Expansion airfields. The drawing number on the site plan is 175/35, but is unconfirmed.

Latrine Block – 230/36 – RAF West Raynham
Concrete version.

Mechanical Transport Sheds and Offices – RAF Shawbury
This was very much the standard Expansion Period design and is believed to be numbered 2782/34. The MT yard was normally made up of two rows of sheds facing each other, one of the rows having the offices to one end. The roof tiles on this one have been replaced recently. The later flat-roofed version could also be seen across the country, Oakington having a fine example which is still in use today.

Mechanical Transport Vehicle Shed – 4501/37 – RAF Silloth
The pump in this shot is probably original.

Mechanical Transport Sheds – RAF Shawbury

Mechanical Transport Sheds – 6234/36 and 5907/36 – RAF Upwood
This picture shows one row of the standard concrete pattern of MT Sheds.

Mechanical Transport Shed – 8047/27 – RAF Hucknall
With modification to left.

Mechanical Transport Sheds (c1916) – RFC Bramham Moor/RAF Tadcaster
This temporary, rudimentary, wood and asbestos sheet construction really has
stood the test of time.

Articulated Trailer Shed – RAF Leconfield
On this one the entrance has been sealed up and the building itself modified to
accommodate a static generator. The ducting to the side is not original.

Fire Fighting Mechanical Transport Shed – 2803/38 ? – RAF Scampton
Believed to be for the storage and maintenance of specialised vehicles and
equipment.

Fire Fighting Mechanical Transport Shed – RAF Waddington
This FFMT shed has been modified to house a social venue. The tiled roof is
also a replacement.

Articulated Trailer Shed – 7328/38 – RAF West Raynham

Armoury – 7616/37 (Bomber Station Type) – RAF Swinderby
Normally one of the largest buildings on the Technical site, this substantial
design was to be found at many bomber airfields. There was also a concrete
version. Many versions had only five windows across the first floor at the front,
compared with seven on others. Bomber armouries had a photographic
section on their first floor. This design was based on the single storey 'Fighter
Station Armoury' 1639/38. These could be upgraded to Bomber standard.

Armoury – 4829/35 – RAF Hemswell
This left side view shows the size of this block. The two doors on the far left
were originally windows. However the building does have three doors together
at the rear, out of view on this shot. Looks identical to the 7616/37.

Gun Turret Instruction Building –
12167/39 and 17722/39 – RAF West Raynham
This design of steel and asbestos sheet building was superseded during the Second World War by the 11023/40. A double version of the earlier design can still be seen at Bicester. See below.

Double Turret Training Building – RAF Bicester
Double version of the above.

Double AML Bombing Teacher – W578/39 – RAF Jurby
The Air Ministry Laboratories Bombing Teacher seen here was a standard
building and could be found at many stations. It is an earlier version of the
6301/42. Many site plans carry differing drawing numbers for this building and
most refer to later modifications.

**Combined AML Bombing Teacher and Turret Trainer –
633/42** – RAF Tatenhill
This was yet another way of cutting down on the use of raw materials during
the war. Putting the buildings together like this obviously saved thousands of
bricks as well as considerable time in erection. Space could also be saved, but
here at Tatenhill this was not a consideration. This 'Hybrid' design was based
on the 1739/41 and the 11023/40.

Link Trainer Building – 12386/38 – RAF Newton
This building was designed to house two 'Link' trainers although many only had one installed. It measured approximately 50' x 20'. Distinguishing features are its double door to the front, with three small windows at either side.

Link Trainer Building – 12386/38 – RAF Leconfield
Rear view of above. The ducting seen on the left is modern.

Link Trainer and Bombing Teacher Building – RAF Ringway
This hybrid design dates from the war years and is thought by many to have been unique. Unfortunately it was demolished in February 1996 to make way for the new British Airways terminal at what is now Manchester Airport.

Link Trainer
This is the type of Link trainer that would actually be housed in many of these buildings. The instructor's control desk can also be seen lower left. Many museums, including Duxford, have specimens of these.

Synthetic Navigation Classroom – 2468/42 – RAF West Raynham
This wartime design was based on the standard Gymnasium 14604/40, but
without the end and side annexes. It would have fulfilled a similar function to
the 'Airmanship Hall', with a more obvious slant towards navigation training.

Navigation Hut – 1852/18 – RAF Duxford
A classroom for training pupils in the art of navigation. Of course, there was no
electronic gadgetry in those days and thus a good grasp of basic navigation
skills was an absolute must.

Station Education Section – 3702/35 – RAF Manby
Many educational functions were fulfilled in this building, including further training/education, promotion training, night school, as well as all the associated exams. The station library could also be housed here. All major stations would have an education block.

Instructional Block – 3217/36 – RAF Manby
This huge building is rare and may have been peculiar to stations with a large training commitment. Unlike the 'Education' block this was basically a college with many classrooms etc used for 'Trade Training'. Apart from the Officers' Mess this is the largest building at Manby and extends far off to the right of this picture.

Training/Education Section – RAF Shawbury
This design was present at a few of the Expansion airfields, including Ternhill. This one here continues in its training and educational role. It now houses the Central Air Traffic Control School HQ and the Air Traffic Control Training Squadron.

Lecture Rooms (circa 1928) – RAF Bicester
This large school had an Armoury (seen lower right) added in the late 1930s.

Gunnery Instruction Hut/Armoury – 293/17 – RAF Duxford

Photographic Hut, Sports Gear Room and Post Office – 504/18
RAF Duxford

Part 3

Living, Communal, Administration and Other Sites

Single Sergeants' Quarters – RAF Leconfield

Wardens Office – 2880/37 – RAF Kirkbride
This small guard room was to be found at dozens of sub-sites.

Guard House and Fire Party (circa 1935) – RAF Shawbury
This large popular design also incorporated the Fire Party with a tender shed
to the left. Many inter-war Guardroom designs would incorporate a Fire Party
with tender shed. Compare this five-arch version with the three-arch version
seen at Manby, opposite.

Guard House – 1621/27 – RAF Hucknall

Guard House – 4534/35 – RAF Manby
The two outer arches have given way to normal windows; I bet 'Jack and Vera' would like the cladding. There is a larger but similar building opposite this one at Manby; it appears in all respects to be a guard house but shows on the site plan as a 4446/35 Fire Party and Post Office.

Guard House and Fire Party – 3799/38 – RAF Jurby
This temporary wooden design has all the features of your normal guardroom
with reception, toilets, cells, offices and fire party accommodation

Guard House with Fire Party – 469/38 – RAF Colerne
Another popular design of the period with many still extant.

Guard House – RAF Sealand
This was one of a handful of guardrooms at Sealand. The station was very large and by 1942 had three camps, East, West and South. Note the similarity in the roof structures between this example and the 166/23 on the next page.

Fire Party House – 3344/37 – RAF Bicester

Guard House – RAF Sealand

Guard House and Fire Party – RAF Upwood
The tender shed is positioned like many, at the right, to the rear.

Guardroom – 166/23 – RAF Bicester
As Bicester expanded during the Expansion Period, the Fire Party section
within this guardroom was found to be inadequate and in 1937 this building
was complemented by a separate 'Fire Party' and tender shed. See next page.

Fire Party and Tender Shed – 1266/32 – RAF Duxford
Viewed from the rear of the guardroom.

Sector Operations Block – RAF Ternhill
Much of this ops block is now demolished. Part of the blast protection walls can still be seen on the left. It would have been the Operational Control Centre for many of the airfields in and around Shropshire. It was fairly uncommon at the time, but this building was dispersed, being situated well to the north of the airfield on the main Whitchurch road. The 'Sector Ops Block' was much larger than the normal block, due to its additional responsibilities.

Operations Block – RAF Bicester
This ops block is from the 1920s and is thought to be the same design as the one at Duxford, a 1161/24 with seven windows at the entrance side and ten at the opposite side. This is however unconfirmed. This one was situated right by SHQ.

Operations Block – 1161/24 (757/27) – RAF Duxford
This was a standard inter-war design and was used throughout the war. The protective earth banks were added during the Second World War. The 757/27 is thought to be referring to a later modification. The young Douglas Bader and his contemporaries would have received their instructions from here. One of the other stations to have an example was Upavon.

Operations Block entrance – 1161/24 (757/27) – RAF Duxford
This picture is included to show some of the added features that were present at many buildings during the war years. The windows were taped, normally in a criss-cross pattern. This would help stop flying glass during a raid. Fire buckets normally containing sand were also on hand to help extinguish any fires. The protective earth banks can be seen on either side.

Station Offices – 352-3/30 – RAF Duxford
This building was normally referred to as the Station HQ. The main station administration would be done here, two of the main functions being records and pay accounts. The Commanding Officer would also have his main office here. At many stations the HQ would be near or opposite the guardroom by the main entrance.

Station Offices – 352-3/30 – RAF Duxford
Rear view of the preceding.

Station HQ – 190/36 – RAF Manby
Many Stations had Headquarters like this one. It is a standard pattern and although it is smaller than the more common 1723/36, it is very similar. Compare the five windows across the first floor frontage with that of the Waddington HQ on the next page. At first glance they both look the same. Of course these HQs, like other buildings could have been traditionally tiled or latterly, the flat roofed protected style.

Station HQ – 1723/36 – RAF Shawbury
These Neo-Georgian arches are to the rear of one of the side annexes and although they appeared on many Expansion buildings, they were by no means standard on the HQ.

Station HQ – 1723/36 – RAF Waddington
Large numbers of Expansion Period airfields had this style of HQ. Amongst them, Upwood, Leeming, Bircham Newton, Leconfield and Oakington. This one has been re-roofed at the sides. This 1723 had an Ops Block annexe to the rear, as was the case at many bomber stations.

Station HQ – 1723/34 – RAF Hemswell
Rear view with Ops Block Annexe to left. Many HQs had various departments
added later, for example Wireless Telegraphy rooms, photographic section and
in some cases an armoury.

Station HQ – 2878/37 – RAF Kirkbride
This 'small' station offices can be seen at MUs. It can be identified by having
seven windows either side of the entrance and is 'E' shaped in plan.

Station HQ and Offices – 1443/24 – RAF Bicester
It is not known if this design was widespread. Very similar patterns can be seen elsewhere. See below.

Station HQ and Offices – 1610-1/26 – RAF Sealand
Larger than the example above but nonetheless very alike. Other later modifications to this example include AMD numbers, 2060-1/26, 249/27 and 1474/27.

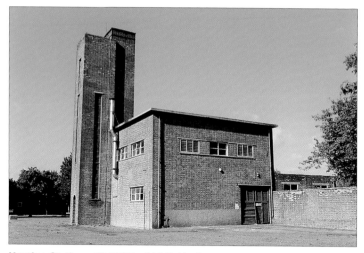

Heating Station – 6217/35 – RAF Oakington
The coal used to fire the boilers would be stored in a large compound right next to this large building. The heating for the station would be supplied from here through a network of pipes. On many a station one can lift the slabs on the paths and see the heating pipes which were ducted beneath. Some larger stations may have two of these heating units. As evident from this picture the 6217/35 had a flat roof and it was a very substantial building indeed. It is probably the most common of the Expansion heating stations.

Central Heating Station – 16004/39 – RAF Colerne
It is not known how this example differs from the 6217/35. It is thought that the number 16004/39 refers to a later refinement. The fuel compound is in the foreground.

Central Heating Station – 2918/36 – RAF Upwood
This was a popular concrete section design. In the foreground is the original brick fuel compound. Later, this heating station, like many others, changed over to being oil-fired and the oil storage tanks can be seen on the left.

Heating Station – 9299/38 – RAF Kirkbride
This was one of the smaller single storey heating stations normally used to supplement an existing one or supply a sub-site. To the left we can see the married wardens quarters 5917/37.

Central Heating Station
RAF Colerne
Another example of the smaller type design.

Photographs on the opposite page:

Standby Set House – RAF Colerne
Seen on the far left of the picture to the rear of the building, are the diesel tanks used to supply the generators.

Standby Set House – 1059/38
RAF Kirkbride

Standby Set House – 10966/3?
RAF West Raynham
This standard type of large concrete Standby Set House was protected like most others, with a blast protective outer wall.

Standby Set House/Power House 11307/38 – RAF Bicester
This large building was used to supply power through two or three diesel generators in the event of a mains failure. Similar designs were utilised across the country, including Duxford, which had a 5590/38.

Standby Set House – 607/36 – RAF Upwood
Here we have another concrete version, but this one is much smaller.

Compressor House – 5044/37 – RAF Silloth

Compressor House – RAF Scampton

Air Raid Shelter (circa 1939) – RAF Shawbury
Thought to be a type of 'Stanton' shelter from the late Expansion Period. This
shelter, like all the other semi-sunken, had a grass covering, with one entrance
and one emergency escape. The escape hatch can be seen nearest the
camera. All sites had their shelters. The one seen above served the Warrant
Officers Quarters.

Air Raid Shelter – RAF Colerne
Again, this shelter situated near the SHQ is believed to be derived from the 'Stanton'.

Air Raid Shelter – RAF Bicester
This shelter is strange in as much as it had squared-off sides to the entrance, which could be an additional hazard when entering in a hurry. Normal entrances had safer sloping sides. See the previous shelter photographs.

Air Raid Shelter – RAF Bicester
Not a strange Machine Gun post as may be first thought, but a rather unusual linear ARS. Just above the grass line can be seen a row of small openings. The entrance was to the rear.

Air Raid Shelter – W439/40 – RAF Jurby
Jurby has many examples of this double entranced shelter. It is half the size again of the normal Stanton types.

Air Raid Shelter (Stanton) – RAF Kirkbride
Internal view.

Air Ministry Works Dept and Water Tower – 7957/38 – RAF Kirkbride
When approaching an RAF station this would often be the first building one would see as it towered over the others. These buildings were covered by many Air Ministry drawing numbers as they were not the same size in every instance, though ostensibly they all looked the same. The design included garages, workshops, tool rooms, pumphouse, purification plant, offices and the like. The buildings surrounded a vehicle and storage compound/yard.

Water Tower – 7957/38 – RAF Silloth
By looking at this now rare pressure gauge (centre right), the amount of water held in the tank would be known.

Air Ministry Works Dept and Water Tower – 5992/36 and 1336/37
RAF West Raynham

Water Tower and Work Services – RAF Newton

High Level Water Tanks
RAF Colerne
The old and the new side by side. The steel tanks on the left were an early war addition to this site at Colerne. This type of water tank, erected high on a steel frame, was a common 1940s airfield feature. The pre-cast concrete tank is a 1990s replacement

High Level Water Tank – 1178/25 (L) and 300,000 gal Reservoir – 730-4/24 (R) – RAF Bicester
Early pre-cast concrete structures.

Borehole Pumphouse and Chlorinator Plant – RAF West Raynham
Many Expansion Period camps had their own water supply and they had the
ability to chlorinate also.

Work Services Building – 1134/27 – RAF Bicester
Duxford also had one of these. Behind the tree is a set of double doors.

Station Gymnasium and Chancel – 14604/40 – RAF St Eval
Compare this standard temporary gym of the war years with the earlier version on
page 90. Virtually all major stations built during the war years had one of these.

Station Gymnasium – RAF Shawbury
Standard gym of the period. Amongst the other stations to have these were
Ternhill. Stations often used dormant hangars as sports halls.

Squash Court – 1420/37 – RAF Leconfield
This design was present at many stations and as can be seen, was flat-roofed.
Other popular designs had a more traditional style of roof with gable ends.
New windows and door have been added.

Grocery Shop and Store – 1427/36 – RAF West Raynham
Originally rectangular in shape, with a store to the rear, this building has been extended to the left and an entrance porch added to the right. Not only fresh groceries could be purchased here, but Brylcreem, starch and boot polish, all of which were important items in any self-respecting airman's arsenal!

Ration Store – RAF Upwood
The ration store was nearly always positioned immediately behind, or very near to the Dining Room or the combined Institute/Dining Room. Compare this one to the smaller 3172/38. These buildings can easily be confused with Guardrooms.

Ration Store – 3172/38 – RAF Colerne
Note only two pillars and the flat roof.

Squash Courts – RAF St Eval
Clad with corrugated sheets, this court resembles closely the naval version which can be seen at Arbroath. It is however thought to be another version of the common wartime RAF design, the 16589/40.

Ration Store – 222/36 – RAF Manby
Traditionally tiled and still showing its wartime camouflage, this example is now used as the local Boy Scout and Girl Guide HQ.

Canteen Block – 2876/37 – RAF Lichfield
Viewed from above this building is 'E' shaped. It can be recognised with its six windows either side of the front door. The windows are not original on this one; one has been replaced by a door on the left. This canteen was provided at MUs.

Canteen Block – 287637 – RAF Kirkbride
Internal view. Note the curved ceiling.

Dining Room – RAF Manby
This large dining room for the lower ranks is believed to be part of drawing number 3013/35, which also includes the Institute which in this instance was positioned immediately behind this building.

Dining Room – 6848/39 – RAF Duxford
This Dining Room was added at Duxford to supplement the existing combined Mess and Institute.

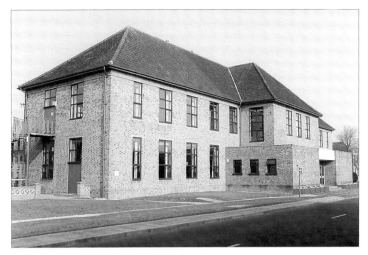

Dining Room – 1680/39 – RAF Waddington
This example is larger than the one at Duxford on the previous page, but it is of a very similar design. Note the modifications to the lower centre section.

Dining Room – RAF Upwood
Flat-roofed version of the above, also with small modifications to the centre section.

Dining Room and Institute – 1482-4/36 – RAF Waddington
Most stations, particularly the later ones, would have only the one dual-purpose
building; this was done for economy and convenience. Many older stations
would be supplemented by a separate Dining Room. The right hand side of this
one was badly damaged during an enemy attack and rebuilt shortly afterwards.

Dining Room and Institute – 1482-4/36 – RAF Shawbury
The example here at Shawbury has had a new roof recently and also evident is
a small modification to the right. The lower ranks Dining Rooms were also
referred to as the 'Airmen's Mess'.

Dining Room and Institute – RAF Upwood
This, like the 1482/36, has the two entrance and stairwell sections protruding from the frontage. In my experience the Mess was nearly always to the right and the NAAFI to the left, when viewed from the front.

Institute and Airmen's Mess – 8055-60/38 – RAF Colerne
Still like many being used for its original purpose, albeit by the army. Note the small round windows and compare with the similar mess on the next page.

Dining Room and Institute – 8055-60/38 – RAF Hemswell
View of rear.

Dining Room and Institute – 8055-60/38 – RAF Hemswell

Dining Room and Institute – 852/32 – RAF Duxford
An earlier 1930s design for 291 corporals and airmen which was later
supplemented by a new Dining Room. The 2896/34 refers to a later
modification. As with most of these type of structures the main features are the
two protruding stairwells to the front.

Institute – RAF Manby
Thought to be from drawing 3013/35, from which the Dining Room is illustrated on page 94.

Institute – 4572/38 – RAF Jurby
This and the view on the top of page 100 show the temporary type of designs from the period. The building seen here also housed the Airmen's Mess and is of Air Ministry timber hutting.

Institute Annexe – 4572/38 – RAF Jurby
Nissen annexe to the Institute.

Barrack Block – 11587/38 – RAF Waddington
This, the smaller of the 'H' blocks would accommodate 8 NCOs and 56 men.
The basic pattern was two accommodation blocks joined in the centre by an
ablution block. Many 'H' blocks, including the 11587/38 and the 1132/38 were
provided with a Basement Refuge (Shelter). The number for this shelter was
2230/39.

Barrack Block – 11587/38 – RAF Oakington
Still with its original flat roof, this 'H' block has seven windows across the first floor frontage as compared with nine on the larger 'H' blocks seen on page 102.

Barrack Block – 1132/38 – RAF Newton
Here we have the larger of the popular 'H' blocks. It was built to house 8 NCOs and 84 airmen. It is more widespread than the 11587/38 and can be seen on many RAF stations.

Barrack Block – 1132/38 – RAF Leconfield
New roof added.

Barrack Block – 1132/38 – RAF Upwood
This side view shows the sort of modifications that can be made besides the addition of a new roof. A side door has been added with a ramp and staircases have also been added, possibly to meet Health and Safety requirements, but more than likely to ease access.

Barrack Block – 444/36 – RAF Scampton
This design is best described as 'half an H'. There were various sizes of which this for three NCOs and 68 airmen was the most abundant. Four windows have been bricked up and a new roof added to this one.

Barrack Block – RAF Shawbury
This picture shows the rear of a 'half H' design believed to be another 444/36.
Like most other buildings at Shawbury it has been re-roofed.

Barrack Block – 1424/26, 1498/26 – RAF Sealand
Four of these remain at Sealand and each has the date '1927' above the main
entrance. The door on the ground floor to the right is a modern modification.
This plain design is fairly representative of the 1920s.

Barrack Block Type 'R' – 2357/36 – RAF Upwood
Another 'half H' pattern, but larger than the 444/36, with 13 windows across the
first floor compared with only 11 on the 444.

Barrack Block Type 'R' – 2357/36 – RAF Upwood
Rear view.

Barrack Block Type 'J' – 74/35 – RAF Manby
Probably the largest of all the Barrack blocks and found at the larger stations including Ternhill. Again this is a 'half H' design. This one was for officers at Manby and as such had a stylish porch added.

Barrack Block Type 'J' – 74/35 – RAF Manby
Rear view showing the added fire escapes.

Barrack Block Type 'B' – 177/35 – RAF Manby
Slightly smaller than the 74/35 it has 11 windows across the first floor, whilst the 74/35 has 13. Seen on the right is a 'J', 74/35 for the Airwomen and has no porch. (see previous page)

Barrack Block (Officers) circa 1916 – RFC South Shotwick
These standard type barracks were used throughout the 1930s and '40s, but as a First World War design the were very basic with few frills. The camps at Shotwick later became RAF Sealand.

Officers' Mess – 3935/35 – RAF Manby
This view shows one of the wings or annexes which is now an 'Eventide' home.

Officers' Mess – 3653/36 – RAF Hullavington
For 98 married Officers and 72 single Officers. At first glance they look just like the 3935/35. However the 3653 has slightly smaller wings and has only four chimney stacks visible at the front. The internal layout is also different.

Officers' Mess with Messmans Quarters – 4570/38 – RAF Jurby
Compare this temporary, timber and brick Mess with the others in this section.

Officers' Mess – 570-572/37 – RAF Upwood
The most common of the Expansion styles, with a three arched entrance and
two storey wings. The 570 seen here has only four windows either side of the
main entrance and is believed to be a later version of the 2948/34 which had
five windows on either side. Examples of both can be seen across the country,
including Duxford which has a 2948/34 modified to 2964/35 and 204/35.
A smaller Mess with only three windows on either side also existed.

Officers' Mess – RAF Waddington
Compare this modified entrance to the others shown in this section. It is still
unmistakable. This one here at 'Waddo' has also been treated to a new roof.

Officers' Mess – RAF Oakington
This example is of the flat-roofed variety and is accepted as being a version of
the 2984/34. At Oakington, the side annexes or wings were 'L' shaped,
compared to the normal, rectangular. Many drawing numbers exist for this
style of Mess. They normally refer to later refinements or size of the annexes.
Sometimes these modifications are internal and so the external look of the
buildings remains unchanged. Other numbers include 8700/37 at Hemswell
and 288-291/34 at Harwell.

Officers' Mess – RAF Newton

Sergeants' Mess – RAF Newton
This large standard Mess had an accommodation annexe either side of the main building.

Sergeants' Mess – 3699/35 – RAF Manby
In common with the large majority of Sergeants' Messes the 3699/35 had one annexe to the left. Occasionally for geographical reasons it was to the right.

Sergeants' Mess – 3484/36 – RAF Upwood
A popular pattern with annexe to the left. The small porch seen on the right is a much later 'add-on'.

Sergeants' Mess – 3484/36 – RAF West Raynham
The side annexe, originally to the left on this one has been demolished.
A feature of this type of Mess is the elongated window above the main entrance.

Single Sergeants' Quarters – 8378/39 – RAF West Raynham
Basically a Sergeants' barrack block, and used to supplement existing accommodation.

Station Sick Quarters – 1963/34 – RAF Manby
This single level 'Medical Centre' is much smaller than the 7503/37 and it is unclear why a large station like Manby had one. Maybe this earlier design was found to be just too small and so the 7503/37 was designed. Waddington also sports a 1963/34 which has been extended.

Station Sick Quarters – 7503-4/37 – RAF Swinderby
This was the most numerous of the SSQ types and fine examples can be seen at many locations. Normally a Decontamination Centre for the 'Wounded' would be adjoining the rear.

Station Sick Quarters – 7503/37 – RAF Newton
Note the decontamination annexe just visible to the rear.

Station Sick Quarters – 7503/37 – RAF Scampton
Many SSQs have had tiled roofs added, as has this one at Scampton.

Decontamination Centre (wounded) – RAF Shawbury
The standard style of Decontamination Centre of the period could be reached
through a corridor from the SSQ. This Decontamination Centre was for the
wounded and as such was an annexe to the SSQ. Other Centres were added
for the 'unwounded', where required. The one depicted has had some of its
blast protection removed and is likely to be from AMD 7503-4/37 or 6224/37.

Decontamination Centre (wounded) – 7503-4/37 – RAF Upwood
The centre would be protected all round by an 'air lock'. Inside would be an
undressing room, showers, eye douching facilities, toilets and dressing room.

Decontamination Centre (unwounded) – 6224/37 – RAF West Raynham
Often situated some way from the SSQ it had two side entrances through the
blast protection.

Decontamination Centre (circa 1939) – RAF Shawbury
This was the standard wartime style and they are still plentiful across the
country. As the perceived need for Decontamination Centres grew, these were
added at many stations to supplement existing facilities. Many drawing
numbers exist, including 13843/40 at Woodhall Spa, 16696/39 at Ringway,
16711/39 at Cranage and 16690/39 at Peterhead. At many of the later wartime
stations the Decontamination Centre at the Sick Quarters was referred to on
their site plan as 'Sick Quarters Annexe', eg Peplow.

Double Decontamination Centre – RAF Shawbury
The double versions had four entrance doors, as compared with the normal
two.

Gas Decontamination Centre Type 'E' – 7074/39 – RAF Silloth
The types 'E', 'F' and 'G' types were smaller and could be found at later
expansion airfields and MUs.

Gas Decontamination Centre Type 'F' – 7075/39 – RAF Lichfield
This one has had its entrances and windows bricked up and painted.

Gas Decontamination Centre (Type 'G'?) – 770/38 – RAF Kirkbride
A 'G' type at Lichfield carries the number 7074/39.

Decontamination Centre (unwounded) – 2425/40 ? – RAF Swinderby

Mortuary – 2794/34 – RAF Manby
This early Expansion Period mortuary was small and differed from most others in that it did not have the attached ambulance garage.

Mortuary and Ambulance Garage – 5703/36 – RAF Syerston
'L' shaped with flat roof. Still surviving the JCB in March 1997.

Mortuary and Ambulance Garage – 5887/36 – RAF Duxford
Tiled roof version.

Airmen's Married Quarters – 2255/34, 4161/35 – RAF West Raynham
My visit to West Raynham gave me an excellent opportunity to have a look
round some MQs that were in good condition, uninhabited and virtually
unmodified. West Raynham's MQs are representative of most stations.

Airmen's Married Quarters – 2255/34 – RAF Hucknall

Warrant Officers' Married Quarters – 193/35? – RAF Shawbury
The garages at either end of these semis are a 1990s addition.

Officers' Married Quarters – 528/39 – RAF West Raynham

Officers' Married Quarters – 2533/36 – RAF West Raynham
Larger than the OMQs seen above and obviously for the high-ranking.

W/T Transmitter Station – 2489/36 – RAF Manby
This radio station was heavily fortified, as is clearly evident.

Mobilisation Store – 748/39 – RAF Jurby

Sewage Site Percolating Filters – 3349/36 – RAF Hemswell
The main features of the sewage site were - Tool house, Destructor house,
Sludge drying beds, Percolating filters and Humus tank.

Sludge Drying Beds – 9538/39 – RAF Hemswell
These large flat rectangular drying beds were always laid in rows next to each
other.

Sewage Site Tool Shed – 8558/39 – RAF Hemswell
This has recently acquired new roof tiles.

x

Sewage Site – RAF Langford Lodge
The building to the right is the Tool house and the one on the left is believed to be the Destructor house.

Bulk Fuel Installation (circa 1937) – RAF Leconfield
This BFI is disused now but still in very good condition. Like many it is only semi-sunken with plenty of earth blast protection. Note the fuel bowser pumps in the foreground. Stations would have up to three of these installations, giving tankage for up to 216,000 gallons, or enough to last for six weeks of intensive operations. The tanks that made up these installations were 9 feet in diameter by 30 feet in length and each would hold 12,000 gallons.

Bulk Fuel Installation – RAF Scampton

Bulk Fuel Installation – 6458/39 Pump – RAF Kirkbride

All the pumps were still *in situ* and looked almost useable.

Bulk Fuel Installation – 6458/39 Fuel Type sign – RAF Kirkbride

INDEX

By Building Type

We hope that you enjoyed this book

Midland Publishing titles are edited and designed by an experienced team of specialists.
Further titles are in preparation though we welcome ideas from authors or readers for books they
would like to see published.

In addition, our associate organisation, Midland Counties Publications, offers an exceptionally
wide range of aviation, spaceflight, astronomy, military, naval and transport books and videos
for sale by mail-order around the world. For a copy of the appropriate catalogue, or to order further copies of this book, please write, telephone, fax or e-mail:

Midland Counties Publications
Unit 3 Maizefield, Hinckley, Leics, LE10 1YF, England
Tel: (+44) 01455 233 747   Fax: (+44) 01455 233 737
E-mail: midlandbooks@compuserve.com